Choose a color. Give it a name. Draw a picture!

the CRAYON MAN

The True Story of the Invention of Crayola Crayons

BY Natascha Biebow
ILLUSTRATED BY Steven Salerno

Clarion Books
An Imprint of HarperCollins*Publishers*
Boston   New York

ONCE there was a man who saw **color** EVERYWHERE.

He noticed the **yellow-orange** petals of the black-eyed Susans in his garden. He marveled at the rich **scarlet-red** tones of the cardinal's feathers. He admired the deep **blue-greens** of the waves in the sea.

Color made him really, really HAPPY!

But ALL DAY LONG at work, all he saw was black.
Black dust,
   black tar,
      black smoke,
         black ink,
            black dye,
               black shoe polish.

His company sold carbon black, a new kind of pigment, or colored substance, made from the soot of burning oil and natural gas. People used it in printing inks, electric street lamps, and stove and shoe polish. It also made rubber car tires last much longer.

His name was Edwin Binney and he was an inventor.

He worked with his cousin C. Harold Smith.
Together they were Binney & Smith.

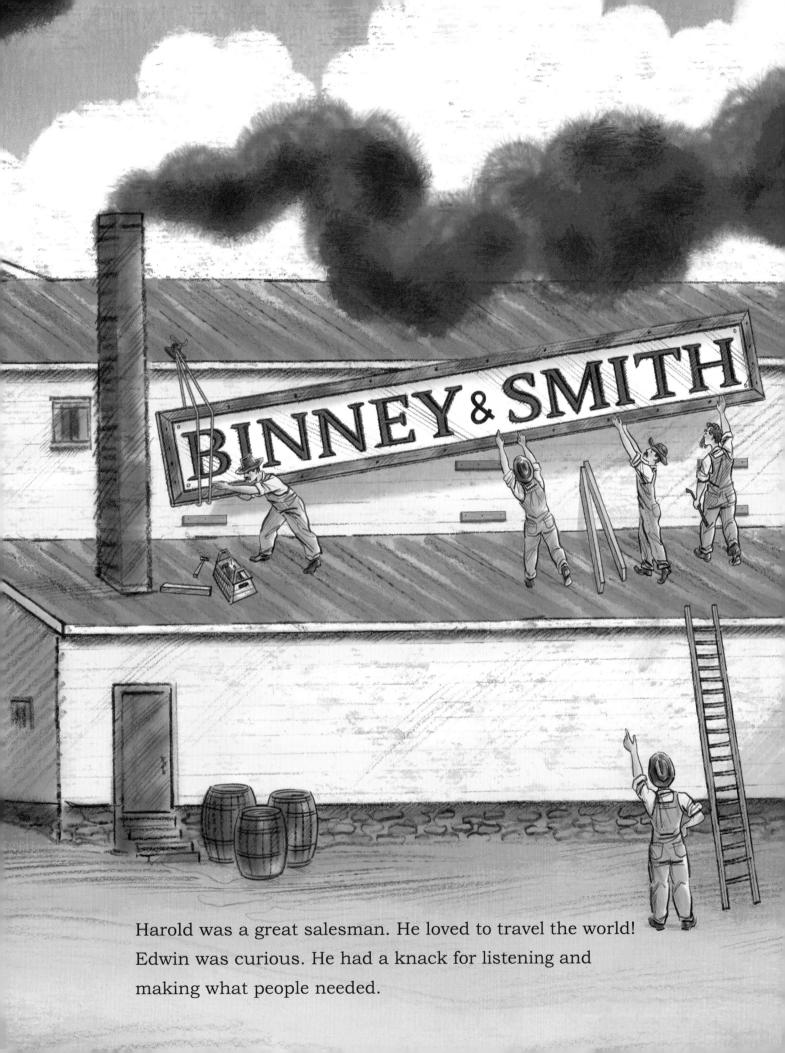

Harold was a great salesman. He loved to travel the world!
Edwin was curious. He had a knack for listening and
making what people needed.

Edwin invented a new kind of inexpensive slate pencil that wrote very smoothly—it was **gray**. Children loved it!

He invented a kind of chalk that wasn't dusty and didn't crumble—it was **white**. Teachers loved it!

He invented a wax crayon that would write on wood and paper packaging. It was really, really **black**. People loved it!

Paper was expensive in the 1800s, so children wrote with slate pencils or chalk on slates (small handheld blackboards).

So when everyone, including Edwin's wife, Alice, told him that children needed better, cheaper crayons, he listened.

They said:

The crayons we have are big, dull, and clumsy.
The lumps of colored clay only make fat, clunky lines.
And the artists' crayons from Europe are far too expensive—
they crumble and break easily.
Some are even poisonous!

Alice used to be a schoolteacher, so she knew what children needed. She encouraged Edwin to invent the crayons.

Edwin thought about his company's inventions:

When you drew a picture with their **gray** slate pencil, it rubbed off at the drop of a hat.

When you drew a picture with their **white** chalk, it smudged everywhere.

If you drew a picture with Edwin's new, really **black** crayon, it was . . . well, really **black**.

None of these inventions was any good for drawing in **color**.

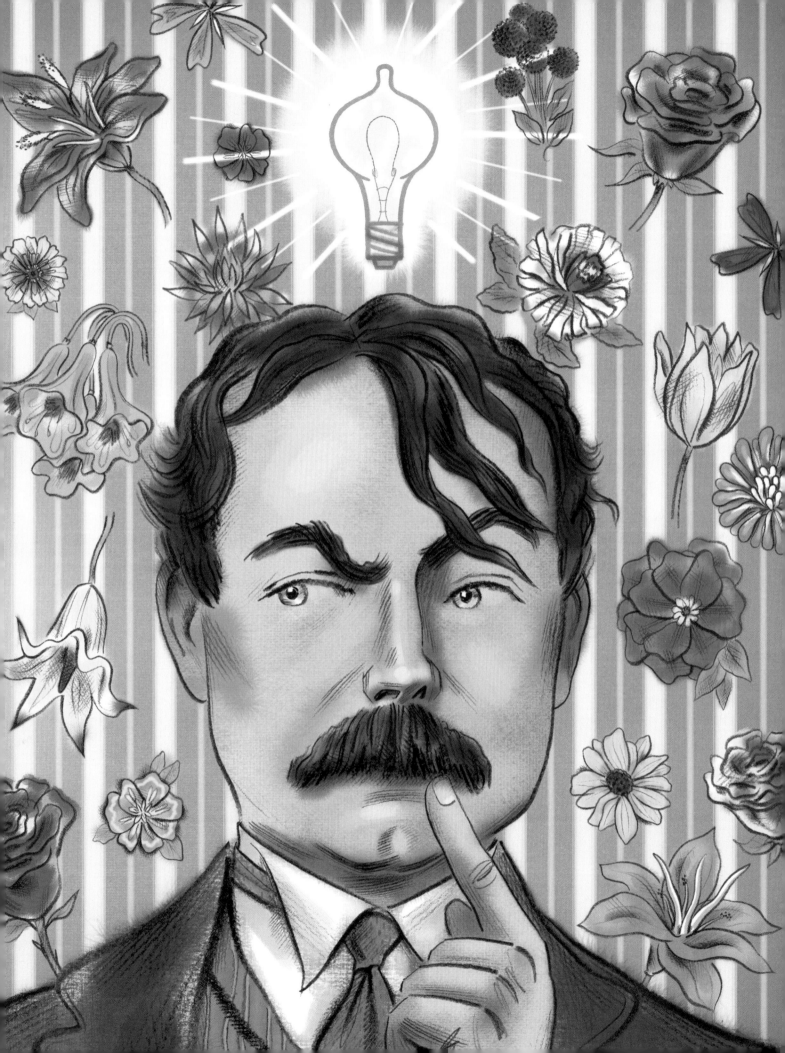

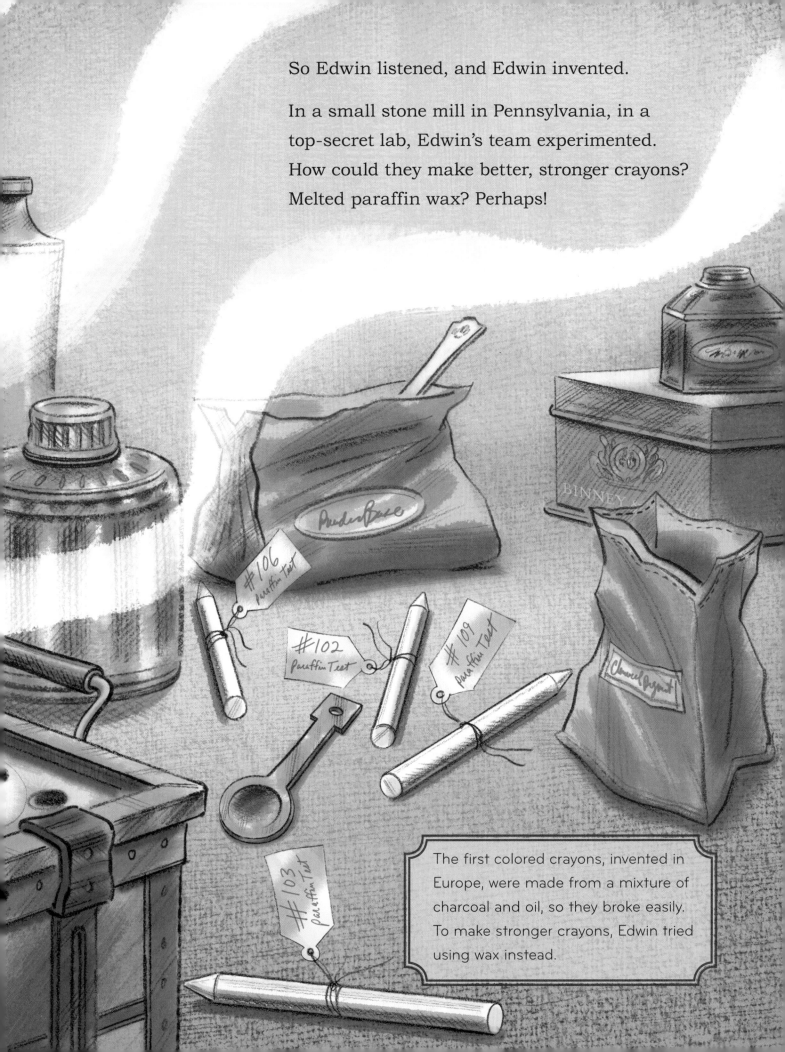

So Edwin listened, and Edwin invented.

In a small stone mill in Pennsylvania, in a top-secret lab, Edwin's team experimented. How could they make better, stronger crayons? Melted paraffin wax? Perhaps!

#106 Paraffin Test

#102 Paraffin Test

#109 Paraffin Test

#103 Paraffin Test

Powder Base

BINNEY

Charcoal Pigment

The first colored crayons, invented in Europe, were made from a mixture of charcoal and oil, so they broke easily. To make stronger crayons, Edwin tried using wax instead.

Now for the crayon colors: grinding, grinding, grinding up rocks and minerals into fine powders.

Mixing, mixing . . . Slate for **gray**. Earth for **yellow**,
red, and **brown**? Perhaps!

Oh, yes, and lapis for **blue**.

Pounding, sifting, and heating the colored powders . . .
Would they be bright enough?

Edwin's team kept on trying.
They kept on experimenting.

Ground-up rocks and minerals made bright
pigments for crayons: red iron oxide (hematite)
for **red**, yellow iron oxide (goethite) for **yellow**,
varied shades of red iron oxide for **brown**, carbon
black for **black**, zinc oxide for **white**, and imported
ultramarine made from lapis lazuli for **blue**.

They came home covered in **color.**

They experimented some more and discovered—

a *pinch* of this pigment,

a *sploosh* of that one,

a little hotter, a little cooler . . .

and *voilà*, **LOTS of different shades**!

Now there were **greens**, **oranges**, **violets**, and **pinks** too!

Edwin came home covered in **color**.

To make **orange**, **green**, and **violet**, chemists blended various pigments and clays. Some minerals changed color when heated. Plus, the length of time the mixtures were left to cool created different colors too.

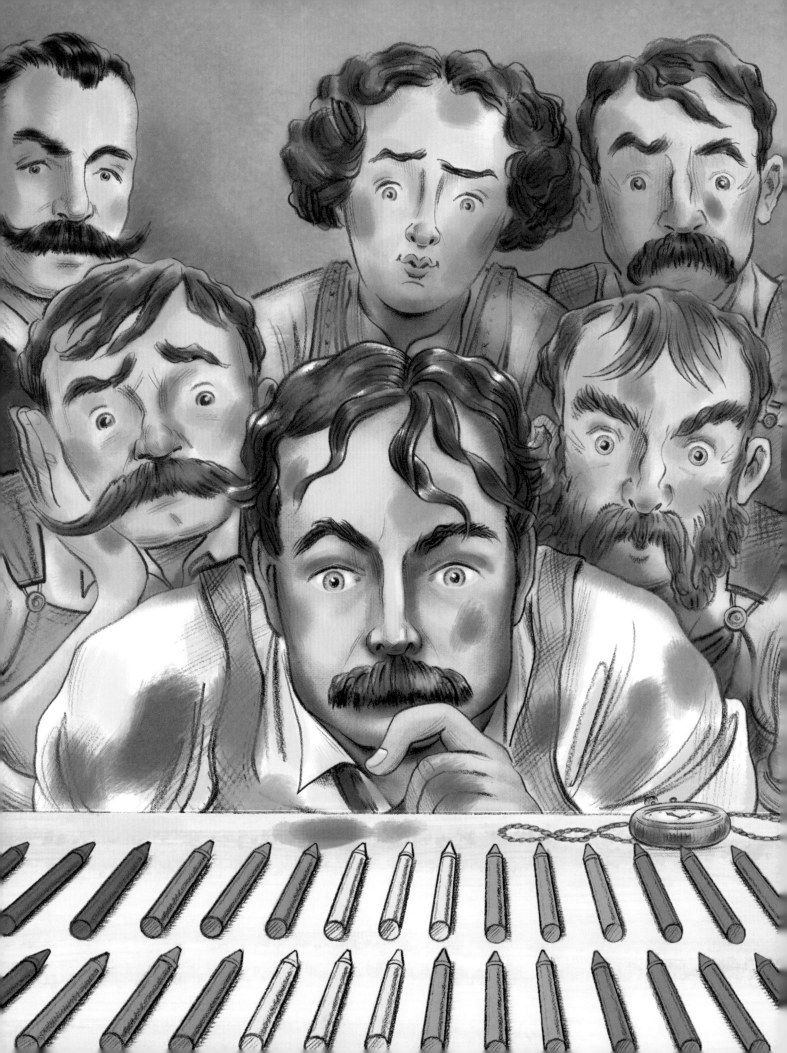

In a large tub at the mill, Edwin's team measured
out the ingredients:
     melted wax,
         clay to thicken,
            something for texture,
             colored powders,
each in *just the right amount* every time to make . . .
a top-secret formula!

Slowly, carefully, stirring by hand, they poured
the special formula into thin, crayon-shaped molds,
smaller than any other inventors'— just the right size
for children's hands.

The mixture cooled and hardened.
Edwin watched, and Edwin waited.

Children might eat or chew the crayons and
get sick, so Edwin's team experimented to
find new safe, nontoxic colors and materials.

Finally, one summer evening in June 1903,
Edwin came home covered in **color**,
and announced that he'd invented
a new kind of colored crayon!

But what should he call it?

Alice had an idea.

She said let's mix the French word *craie*
for stick of chalk, and the word *ola*
from the word *oleaginous,*
meaning oily like the oily texture
of the crayon wax, to invent a new word—

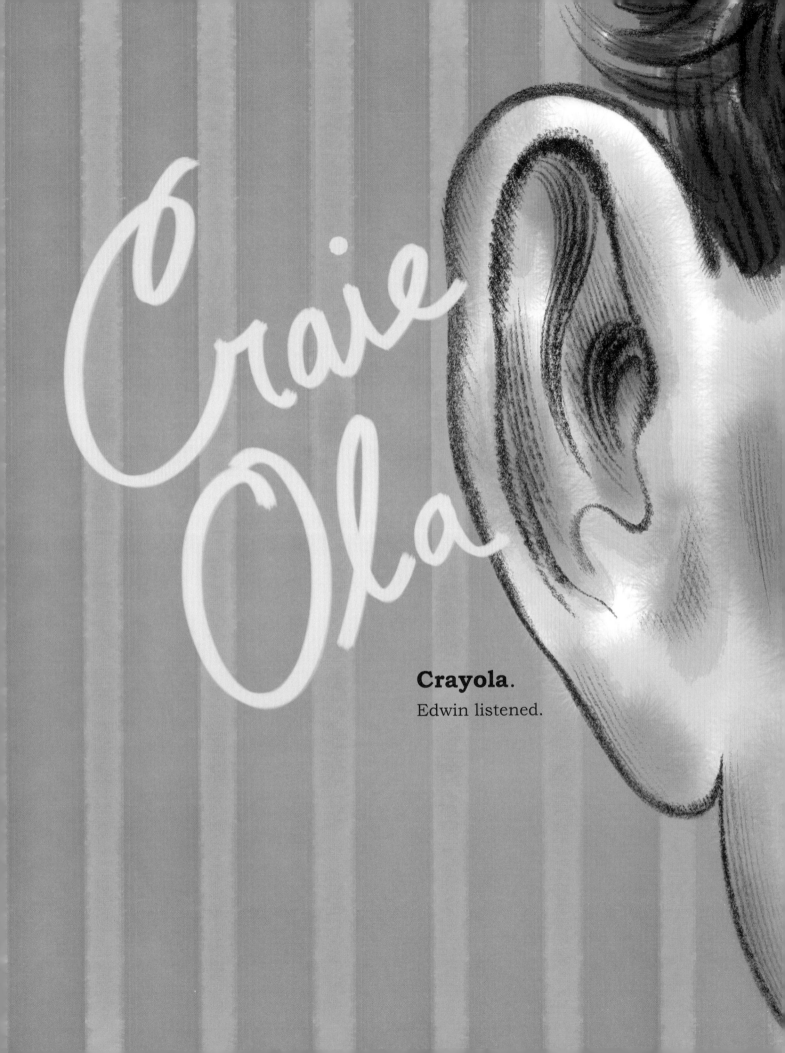

Crayola.

Edwin listened.

Binney & Smith shipped out the first Crayola crayon boxes: **red**, **orange**, **yellow**, **green**, **blue**, **violet**, **brown**, and **black**— eight colored crayons for only a nickel.

Edwin waited.

Would children like them?

Children did!

Now they could draw a tiny **green** caterpillar or the big **blue** sky.
Their drawings wouldn't smudge and they wouldn't rub out.
They were bright and could last a long, long time.

By the 1900s, inventors had figured out how to make cheaper paper from wood pulp, so children could now draw on paper instead of just slate.

Excitement over the new, colorful invention spread like wildfire. Admirers from far and wide flocked to marvel at Binney & Smith's inventions at the St. Louis World's Fair. The company's dustless chalk even won a gold medal! Proudly, Edwin and Harold showed it off, especially on their new Crayola crayon boxes.

Every day, Edwin brought colorful bouquets
from his garden to inspire the Crayola team.

They made crayons in **even more different shades**,
and later asked children to help name some of them.

To celebrate their ninetieth anniversary,
Crayola held a color-naming competition.
The six-year-old winner coined "tropical rain
forest." Other color names created by children
included "robin's egg blue," "tickle me pink,"
and "macaroni and cheese."

At last, because of Edwin Binney, the man who saw **color** everywhere, who had a knack for listening and making what people needed, children all around the world could reach for just the right shade . . .

sunglow!   wisteria!   jungle green!

screamin' green!   razzmatazz!   robin's egg blue!

wild watermelon!   mauvelous!

purple mountains' majesty!   cadet blue!

lavender!   timberwolf!

to draw . . .

ANYTHING!

How Crayola Crayons Are Made Today

In 1903, Crayola crayons were made carefully in small lots, labeled and packed into boxes by hand, and sold to schools. Today, machines produce an average of 12 million crayons a day—that's over 8,333 crayons a minute—in more than 120 different colors! They are sold in over 80 countries around the world.

Train cars deliver paraffin wax to the Crayola factory in Easton, Pennsylvania. The wax is heated, and the clear, melted liquid is stored in tall silos, ready to be pumped inside.

Workers pour colored powders, called pigments, into vats filled with the liquid wax, add clay to thicken it, then mix.

The wax-pigment mixture is pumped into a huge mold. It looks like a giant circular muffin tin! The mix fills all the 110 small crayon-shaped holes in each section.

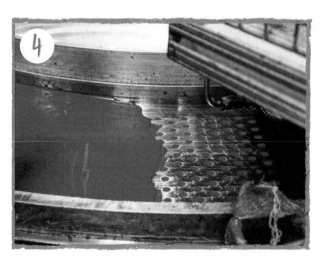

Cold water flows underneath the mold to cool the wax and harden it into crayon shapes. A large blade scrapes off extra wax to be reused later.

The crayons are pushed up from the mold. A robotic arm then moves them to the labeling machine.

Preprinted sticky labels on a huge drum are wrapped around each crayon two and a half times.

Workers check the finished crayons and store them in large cardboard cartons, one for each color.

To make up the Crayola crayon boxes, workers place the crayons in the right order in the collating machine. A chute drops one of each color needed onto a conveyor belt.

A robotic arm opens the flat-packed green-and-yellow Crayola boxes and sends them out onto the conveyor belt. Another arm pushes the collated crayons into each box and closes it.

The boxes move down the conveyor belt to be packed into larger cartons. Crayola ships the finished crayons to the store, and they are sold to you!

A Man Who Loved Color

EDWIN BINNEY was born in 1866. As a child, he loved swimming, hunting, fishing, and sailing. When he grew up and had to work in an office in the city, Edwin decided to build a house on some farmland by the sea in Old Greenwich, Connecticut. He planted a colorful vegetable and flower garden. Most mornings, he walked to the station with his daughters, listening for birdsong. He wanted them to share his love of color and nature too!

"My great-grandfather Edwin Binney was a gentle, kind, and generous man. A passionate lover of nature, Grandpa Bub rarely chose to be indoors, preferring the woods, the wind, the sea, and of course, his much beloved Crayola flower garden, from which he cut and carried bouquets of color to his office each day." —Sally Putnam Chapman, Edwin's great-granddaughter

Funny and bighearted, Edwin kept on listening and creating all his life; but of all his inventions, he loved the Crayola crayons most of all. His partner, C. Harold Smith, was the outgoing salesman, while Edwin worked at the factory with chemists and designers to create their products.

The successful Crayola crayon business meant that Edwin and Harold could give back to the community. Edwin created a big park with flowers, trees, a pond, and playing fields in Old Greenwich. And when times were tough during the

Great Depression, Crayola factory workers kept their jobs and local farmers got work labeling and packing crayons.

After Edwin died in 1934, Crayola continued his mission to create innovative products that bring the wonder of color to people of all ages.

Edwin's wife, Alice, with two of her grandchildren

SELECTED BIBLIOGRAPHY

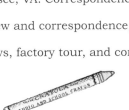

PRIMARY SOURCES:

Print

Awards to Exhibitors and Collaborators at the Universal Exposition 1904: Department D—Manufactures. St. Louis: Louisiana Purchase Exposition, 1904: 183.

Binney, Helen Kitchel. "My Wilderness: Early Childhood Memories." *Memories,* 1st ed. Privately printed. 1979: 1–2, 39.

Binney & Smith Inc., Records, 1897–1998, #624. Archives Center, National Museum of American History, Smithsonian Institution, Washington DC.

Binney & Smith Inc. *The Story of a Rainbow,* 3rd ed. New York: Binney & Smith Inc., 1956 and 1961.

Falco, Marie C. *Mr. Binney as I Knew Him.* Privately printed. October 1941.

Interviews & Correspondence

Hoover V, Charles E. President of the Hoover Color Corporation, Hiwassee, VA. Correspondence, 2015.

Putnam Chapman, Sally. Edwin Binney's great-granddaughter. Interview and correspondence, 2015–17.

Zebley, Eric. Crayola Corporate Communications, Easton, PA. Interviews, factory tour, and correspondence, 2015–17.

SECONDARY SOURCES:

Books & Articles

Crayola. *Colorful Moments in Time.* Easton, PA: Crayola. Printed flier.

Crayola. *How Crayola Crayons Are Made.* Easton, PA: Crayola. Printed flier.

Gillis, Jennifer Blizin. *Edwin Binney: The Founder of Crayola Crayons, Lives and Times.* Chicago: Heinemann Library, 2005.

Junior League of Greenwich. "Rocklyn." *The Great Estates: Greenwich, Connecticut, 1880–1930.* Canaan, NH: Phoenix Publishing, 1986: 42–45.

Oz, Charles. *How Is a Crayon Made?* New York: Simon and Schuster Books for Young Readers, 1988.

Py-Lieberman, Beth. "The Colors of Childhood." *Smithsonian,* November 1999: 32–36.

Websites

"Binney & Smith Inc. History." Funding Universe. (www.fundinguniverse.com/company-histories/binney-smith-inc-history; accessed May 7, 2015).

Crayola. "History." (www.crayola.com/about-us/company/history.aspx; accessed May 7, 2015).

Welter, Ed. "The Definitive History of the Colors of Crayola: Part 1." CrayonCollecting.com. (www.crayoncollecting.com/ccolor01.htm; accessed June 1, 2015).

Welter, Ed. "The History of Crayons: Parts 2–5." CrayonCollecting.com. (www.crayoncollecting.com/hoc02.htm; accessed June 1, 2015).

Videos

"How People Make Crayons." *Mister Rogers' Neighborhood,* episode 1481, "Competition," directed by Hugh Martin, written by Fred Rogers, aired June 1, 1981, on PBS. (pbskids.org/rogers/video_crayons.html).

Rahman, Khaleda, and Bryan Derballa (photographer). "Every Child's Dream, Every Wall's Nightmare! Inside the Colorful Crayola Factory Where 12 Million Crayons Are Made Every Day." *Daily Mail* online. March 2, 2015. (www.dailymail.co.uk/news/article-2974653/Waxing-lyrical-Inside-colourful-Crayola-factory-12million-crayons-100-000lbs-paraffin-wax-day.html).

ACKNOWLEDGMENTS

The author gratefully acknowledges the following people, without whom this book would not have been possible: Edwin Binney's great-granddaughter, Sally Putnam Chapman; Eric Zebley, Andrea Lass, and the team at Crayola; Nancy Bennett, president, St. Lucie Historical Society; Beth Py-Lieberman, museums editor, Smithsonian Institution, Washington, DC; Alison Oswald, American history archivist, and Debbie Schaefer-Jacobs, associate curator, Division of Home and Community Life, at the National Museum of American History, Smithsonian Institution, Washington, DC; Linda White, head librarian, Perrot Memorial Library, Greenwich, Connecticut; Christopher Shields, curator of library and archives, Greenwich Historical Society; Jason D. Stratman, assistant reference librarian, Missouri History Museum Library and Research Center; Chuck Hoover at Hoover Color Corporation; Kristen Fulton; the May 2015 Nonfiction Archaeology course students; my talented editor, Ann Rider, and the team at HMH; my lovely agent, Victoria Wells Arms, SCBWI, and my family.

For my dad, generous entrepreneur,
and my mum, who always believed in me —N.B.

For all the budding young artists who pick up a brush
or pencil or crayon—doodling, drawing, dreaming . . . —S.S.

The illustrations in this book were done in charcoal crayon, gouache, and digital color.
The text type was set in Bookman Oldstyle.

LIBRARY OF CONGRESS CATALOGING-IN-PUBLICATION DATA
Names: Biebow, Natascha, author. | Salerno, Steven, illustrator.
Title: The crayon man : the true story of the invention of Crayola crayons /
by Natascha Biebow ; illustrated by Steven Salerno.
Description: Boston : HarperCollins Publishers, 2019. | Audience: Ages 6-9. | Audience: K to Grade 3.
| Includes bibliographical references.
Identifiers: LCCN 2018034241 | ISBN 9781328866844 (hardback)
Subjects: LCSH: Binney, Edwin—Juvenile literature. | Industrialists—United States—Biography—Juvenile literature.
| Binney & Smith Co.—Juvenile literature. | Crayons—Juvenile literature.
| BISAC: JUVENILE NONFICTION / Technology / Inventions.
| JUVENILE NONFICTION / Biography & Autobiography / Art. | JUVENILE NONFICTION /
Biography & Autobiography / Science & Technology. | JUVENILE NONFICTION /
Boys & Men. | JUVENILE NONFICTION / Business & Economics.
Classification: LCC NC870 .B54 2019 | DDC 741.2/3--dc23
LC record available at https://lccn.loc.gov/2018034241

Manufactured in China | 22 SCP 15 14 13 12 11 10 9 8

Choose a color. Give it a name. Draw a picture!